USBORNE

PARTY CAKES

TO BAKE & DECORATE

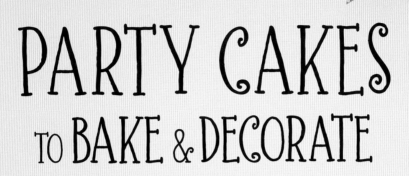

PARTY CAKES
TO BAKE & DECORATE

Abigail Wheatley

Designed by Helen Edmonds & Emma Latham

Illustrated by Francesca Carabelli
Photography by Howard Allman

Recipe consultant: Catherine Atkinson
Food preparation by Maud Eden

Contents

Getting started

The tips on this page will help you to get to grips with some baking basics. Once you've read through them, you can start cooking.

Before you start

Before you start cooking, read the recipe carefully and check you've got all the ingredients and equipment you need. Then, wash your hands.

Weighing & measuring

The recipes show two different types of weights. Use either, but don't swap between them.

For some ingredients, you only need a pinch – the amount you can pick up between your thumb and first finger.

When you measure with a spoon, the ingredients should lie level with the top.

Your oven

All ovens are different – yours may cook things more quickly or slowly than the recipe says. If you're using a fan oven, shorten the cooking time or lower the temperature – the oven manual will help you with this.

Bake cakes in the middle of the oven. Arrange the shelves before you turn on the oven. Only open the oven door when the cooking time is up, or if you think something is burning.

Butter & margarine

To soften butter, leave it at room temperature for an hour before you start cooking. If a recipe says to use margarine, you could use a dairy-free type. Check your margarine is suitable for baking, and avoid 'low fat' types.

Food allergies

If you're cooking for someone with a food allergy or intolerance, this book will help you. Recipes that contain nuts are clearly marked. The ingredients lists show where some allergy-free alternatives can be substituted, and on page 64 you can find out which recipes are suitable for allergy sufferers.

Baking basics

Baking cakes isn't difficult, as long as you follow the recipe. Measure the ingredients as accurately as you can and use the size and shape of cake tin the recipe says. Then, you should bake perfect party cakes every time.

Greasing & lining tins & trays

For greasing, dip a paper towel into softened butter or cooking oil. Rub it over the inside of the tin or tray.

To line a tin or tray, put it on some baking parchment. Draw around it. Cut out the shape. Put it in the tin or on the tray.

Breaking eggs

Crack the egg sharply on the edge of a cup or bowl. Pull the shell apart, so the white and yolk slide into the cup or bowl. Pick out any bits of shell.

Beating eggs

Beat the yolk and white with a fork, to mix them together well.

Separating eggs

1 Break the egg (see above), but let the white and yolk slide onto a small plate.

2 Cover the yolk with an egg cup. Hold the egg cup. Hold the plate over a bowl. Tip, so the white slides in.

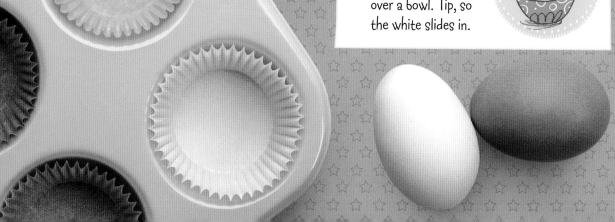

Beating butter & sugar

1 Put the sugar and butter in a big bowl. Stir them together with a wooden spoon.

2 Beat very quickly with the spoon, until the mixture is pale and fluffy.

3 If it's hard to beat, pour hot water into a fresh bowl. Pour it out, dry the bowl, then transfer the mixture to it and try again.

Is it cooked?

At the end of the cooking time, take the cake out of the oven and test it to see if it's cooked.

If the recipe says to test with a skewer, poke a clean skewer into the middle of the cake. Pull it out again. If there is wet cake mix on the skewer, bake the cake for 10 minutes more, then test again.

If the recipe says to test with a finger, poke the middle of the cake quickly with your finger. It should feel firm and springy. If it doesn't, bake for 10 minutes more, then test again.

Mixing gently, or 'folding'

1 Use a spatula or a big metal spoon. Move it gently through the mixture, making the shape of a number 8.

2 Stop as soon as everything is mixed together.

Removing cakes from tins

To remove a cake from a tin with a loose base, undo any clips. Put the tin over a full food

can. Press the sides of the tin down. Then, slide the cake off the base of the tin, onto a plate.

To remove a cake from a tin with a fixed base, run a knife around the edge of the tin. Hold the tin upside down over a wire rack and shake. The cake should pop out.

Sweetie cake

Ingredients:

15g (½oz) unsalted butter

1 lemon

225g (8oz) softened butter or margarine

300g (11oz) caster sugar

6 medium eggs

350g (12oz) plain flour

1 teaspoon baking powder

½ teaspoon bicarbonate of soda

300ml (½ pint) lemon-flavoured yogurt

For decorating:

225g (8oz) icing sugar

food dye (optional)

sweeties, preferably fruit-flavoured

You will also need a fluted ring-shaped cake tin with a capacity of at least 2.5 litres (5 pints) and a pastry brush. To measure capacity, fill the tin with water then measure it into a jug.

Makes around 20 slices

Other shapes

You can use a 20cm (8in) round, deep tin. Grease and line the tin. Halve the quantities. Bake for 30-40 minutes. Cool and ice the cake, then pile the sweeties on top.

This recipe is for a ring-shaped cake with a fruity flavour. When the cake is finished, you ice it and fill the middle of the ring with sweeties.

1 Melt the unsalted butter in a small pan over a gentle heat. Brush it all over the inside of the tin. Measure out all the ingredients. Heat the oven to 180°C, 350°F or gas mark 4.

2 Grate the zest from the outside of the lemon using the small holes of a grater. Squeeze the juice from the lemon.

3 Put the zest, butter or margarine and sugar in a big bowl. Beat until fluffy. Break an egg into a cup. Tip it into the bowl. Add 1 teaspoon of the flour. Mix well.

4 Add each of the remaining eggs the same way. Sift in the rest of the flour, the baking powder and the bicarbonate of soda.

5 Start mixing. When the flour is half mixed in, add the yogurt. Fold everything together gently until just mixed.

The top of the cake may crack but this doesn't matter.

6 Scrape the mixture into the tin. Bake for 45-50 minutes, or until risen and firm. Then, test with a skewer to see if it's cooked (see page 7).

7 Put the tin on a wire rack for 15 minutes, then turn the cake out of the tin onto the wire rack. Leave it to cool completely.

8 To make the icing, sift the icing sugar into a bowl. Add 2½ tablespoons of the lemon juice and a few drops of food dye. Mix.

Other flavours

For a vanilla cake, leave out the lemon and use plain natural yogurt mixed with 2 tablespoons of vanilla essence. For the icing, replace the lemon juice with 1½ tablespoons of water and 1 teaspoon of vanilla essence.

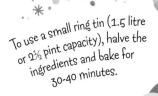

9 Spoon the icing over the cake, so it dribbles down the sides. Pour the sweeties into the middle of the ring.

To use a small ring tin (1.5 litre or 2½ pint capacity), halve the ingredients and bake for 30-40 minutes.

Very chocolatey cupcakes

Ingredients:

1½ tablespoons milk

¼ teaspoon lemon juice

65g (2½oz) rice flour

2 tablespoons cocoa powder

½ teaspoon baking powder
   (gluten-free types are available)

a pinch of bicarbonate of soda

125g (4½oz) caster sugar

65g (2½oz) plain or milk chocolate

65g (2½oz) butter

1 medium egg

For the white chocolate cream:

150g (5oz) white chocolate

25g (1oz) unsalted butter

75ml (3floz) double cream

You will also need a baking tray, around 60 tiny paper cake cases and a piping bag or gun fitted with a star-shaped nozzle.

Makes around 30

This is a paper baking cup. Use it like an ordinary paper cake case.

These little chocolate cakes are moist, rich and wheat- and gluten-free. They're topped with white chocolate cream and home-made chocolate decorations.

1 Heat the oven to 170°C, 325°F or gas mark 3. Put 30 tiny paper cases onto the baking tray. Then, put a second case inside each one. Pour the milk into a jug and stir in the lemon juice.

2 Sift the rice flour, cocoa, baking powder and bicarbonate of soda into a large bowl. Add the sugar and stir.

3 Break up the chocolate. Put it in a pan. Add the butter and 1½ tablespoons of cold water. Heat gently until the chocolate and butter melt.

4 Break the egg into a cup and beat it with a fork. Stir it into the mixture in the jug. Then, pour the mixture into the big bowl.

5 Add the chocolate mixture too. Stir until smooth. Spoon into the paper cases. Bake for 15 minutes, then test with a skewer – see page 7.

6 Leave the cakes for 5 minutes, then move them to a wire rack to cool. Meanwhile, make the white chocolate cream.

7 Break up the chocolate and put it in a bowl. Put the butter and cream in a small pan. Heat gently until the butter melts. Pour the hot cream onto the chocolate.

8 Leave for 2 minutes, then stir until the chocolate melts. Refrigerate for 30 minutes, or until it's like soft butter. Then, beat it with a whisk until pale and fluffy, like whipped cream.

9 Spoon it into your piping gun or bag. Pipe a swirl onto each cupcake, following the instructions on page 52. Add chocolate shapes or sprinkles.

To make chocolate stars or hearts like these, follow the instructions on page 45.

This cupcake was topped with plain chocolate cream – see the box below.

Other flavours

To make plain or milk chocolate cream, you will need 150g (5oz) plain or milk chocolate and 75ml (3floz) double cream. Follow steps 7-9, but leave out the butter.

Icing basics

The recipes in this book use different types of icings, frostings and toppings. Whichever you make, these basic tips will help you. You'll find help with more advanced techniques, such as piping swirls, on pages 52-53.

Icing a cake

Many of the cakes in this book have buttercream or frosting spread on top, and sometimes also around the sides. These tips show you how to do this.

1 Using a blunt knife, scoop up a little frosting or buttercream. Spread it in a thin layer onto the side of the cake. It will make a small patch.

2 Scoop up some more and spread it on next to the first patch. Carry on until the sides are covered.

3 Cover the top of the cake in the same way. When all the cake is covered, wipe the knife blade to clean it.

4 Holding the knife horizontally, run it over the top of the cake, to get the frosting as smooth as possible.

5 Wipe the knife again. Holding it vertically, run it over the sides of the cake, to smooth the frosting.

6 If you prefer a peaky topping, make up-and-down and side-to-side swirling shapes with the knife as you smooth it over the top and sides.

Drippy toppings

Some of the cakes in this book are topped with runny chocolate or glacé icing that drips down the sides. These tips will help you.

1 Spoon on the topping. Use the back of the spoon to spread it out in a thin layer, going right to the edge of the cake.

2 Keep spreading, so a little topping spills over the edge of the cake and drips down the sides. Do this all the way around the edge.

Filling a piping gun

First, attach a nozzle. Then, stand the gun nozzle-end down in a mug or glass. Spoon in some frosting until it is full. Then, attach the plunger to the gun.

Filling a piping bag

1 Push a piping nozzle down to the pointed end of the piping bag. If you're using a plastic piping bag, you may need to snip the end off first.

2 Stand the bag point-down in a mug or glass. Open up the bag and turn over the top edge. This will help to keep it open while you fill it.

3 Spoon in some frosting. Stop when the bag is half full. Unfold the top edge. Make a twist in the bag just above the frosting. Now you are ready to pipe.

Ordinary liquid food dye is fine for tinting icing or buttercream in pale shades, but too much can make the icing or buttercream runny. For strong shades, use gel food dye instead.

To find out how to make piped decorations like this heart, see page 45.

Piping lines or dots

You will need some writing icing, or a filled tube, gun or bag fitted with a tiny round nozzle.

1 For a dot, squeeze until a dot of icing comes out. Stop squeezing and lift the nozzle away quickly.

2 For a line, keep squeezing as you move the nozzle along, leaving a trail of icing. To finish, stop squeezing and lift the nozzle away quickly.

Marshmallow & chocolate cake

Ingredients:

150g (5oz) self-raising flour

40g (1½oz) cocoa powder

2 teaspoons baking powder

200g (7oz) softened butter

200g (7oz) soft dark brown sugar

5 medium eggs

2 teaspoons vanilla essence

4 tablespoons milk

For the topping and filling:

240ml (8floz) double or
whipping cream

1½ tablespoons icing sugar

1 teaspoon vanilla essence

around 350g (12oz) mini
marshmallows

You will also need a 20cm (8in)
round, deep cake tin.

Makes 12-16 slices

This delicious chocolate cake is cut into two layers and then filled and topped with whipped cream and lots of mini marshmallows.

1 Heat the oven to 180°C, 350°F or gas mark 4. Grease and line the tin. Sift the flour, cocoa and baking powder into a bowl.

2 Put the butter and the sugar in a big bowl. Beat until fluffy.

3 Break an egg into a cup. Tip it into the butter and sugar mixture. Add 1 tablespoon of the flour mixture. Beat well. Do this with each egg.

Move the spoon in the...

...shape of a number 8.

4 Mix in the vanilla and milk. Add the rest of the flour mixture. Fold in gently, using a big spatula or metal spoon.

5 Scrape the mixture into the tin. Level the top with the back of a spoon. Bake for 40-45 minutes. Test with a skewer to see if it's cooked.

When the cake is cold, peel off the parchment.

6 Leave it in the tin for 10 minutes. Remove the tin. Put the cake on a wire rack to cool.

These are multicoloured marshmallows, but you could use ordinary pink and white ones.

Other ideas

You could use ordinary marshmallows instead of mini ones.

Or, replace the whipped cream with milk chocolate cream (page 11) and use malted chocolate balls instead of marshmallows.

7 When the cake is cool, put it on a board. Carefully cut it into two layers with a sharp knife. Put the bottom layer on a serving plate.

Don't beat too much, or it will go hard.

8 For the topping, pour the cream into a big bowl. Add the icing sugar and vanilla. Whisk very quickly, until it stays in a floppy point when you lift up the whisk.

9 Spread half the cream over the bottom layer of cake. Scatter on some marshmallows. Put the top of the cake back on. Spread the rest of the cream all over the top and sides of the cake.

10 Starting at the bottom of the cake, arrange the mini marshmallows in rows around the sides, pressing them gently into the cream. Arrange more on the top.

Multicoloured meringues

Ingredients:

2 medium eggs
1 pinch cream of tartar (optional)
100g (4oz) caster sugar
sugar sprinkles
different food dyes

You will also need 2 large baking trays.

Makes around 18

These little meringues are crisp on the outside and chewy on the inside. They are decorated with bright swirls of food dye and sugar sprinkles.

1 Heat the oven to 110°C, 225°F or gas mark ¼. Line the trays with baking parchment – see page 6.

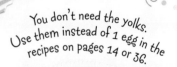

You don't need the yolks. Use them instead of 1 egg in the recipes on pages 14 or 36.

2 Crack one egg on the side of a bowl. Open the shell and let the egg slide onto a plate. Cover the yolk with an egg cup.

3 Hold the plate and egg cup over a big, clean bowl. Tip the plate, so the egg white slides into the bowl. Separate the other egg in the same way.

4 Sprinkle the cream of tartar over the egg whites. Whisk them very quickly with a whisk.

5 Keep whisking until they are really thick and foamy. The egg whites should stay in a stiff point when you lift up the whisk.

6 Add a heaped teaspoon of the sugar. Whisk it in well. Keep whisking in spoonfuls of sugar, until you have used it up.

7 Scoop up a heaped teaspoon of the mixture. Use another spoon to push it onto a tray. Fill the tray with more blobs. Scatter on the sugar sprinkles.

Don't mix the dye in.

8 Spoon the remaining mixture into 3 clean bowls. Dot drops of different food dyes over the mixture in each bowl. Put a blob of mixture on the second tray.

9 Swirl the back of the spoon around the outside of the blob, to make the food dye swirly. Fill the tray with more blobs in the same way.

10 Bake for 40 minutes. Turn off the oven and leave them inside for 15 minutes. Then, take them out and leave them on the trays to cool.

Other ideas

You could sandwich together pairs of meringues with 150ml (¼ pint) double cream, whisked until it stands in a floppy point when you lift up the whisk.

Apricot sprinkle cakes

Ingredients:

1 orange

150g (5oz) ready-to-eat dried apricots

150g (5oz) caster sugar

150g (5oz) softened butter

3 medium eggs

2 teaspoons baking powder (gluten-free types are available)

150g (5oz) semolina or fine cornmeal (polenta)

150g (5oz) ground almonds

For the apricot cream:

300ml (½ pint) double or whipping cream

2 tablespoons smooth apricot jam
red and yellow food dye

sugar sprinkles

You will also need a 12-hole deep muffin tin and a piping gun or bag fitted with a medium star-shaped nozzle.

Makes 12

These moist little cakes contain dried apricots and are covered with apricot cream and sugar sprinkles. You can make them wheat- and gluten-free – see page 64.

1 Heat the oven to 180°C, 350°F or gas mark 4. Grease the inside of each hole of the muffin tin (see page 6).

2 Grate the zest from the outside of the orange using the small holes of a grater. Then, squeeze the juice from the orange.

3 Using kitchen scissors, cut the apricots into small pieces. Put them in a bowl. Add the orange zest and juice.

4 Put the sugar and butter in a big bowl. Beat with a wooden spoon until pale and fluffy.

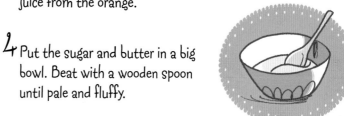

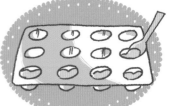

5 Break an egg into a cup, then tip it into the buttery mixture. Mix it in. Do the same with the other eggs.

Don't worry if it looks lumpy.

6 Put the baking powder, semolina or cornmeal and ground almonds in a bowl. Mix. Tip into the big bowl. Add the apricots, juice and zest. Mix well.

7 Spoon the mixture into the holes of the muffin tin. Bake for 20-25 minutes, until risen and firm. Leave for 10 minutes, then turn the cakes onto a wire rack. Leave to cool completely.

8 For the apricot cream, pour the cream into a big bowl. Add the jam and a few drops of food dye. Whisk until it thickens. It should stay in a floppy peak when you lift the whisk.

9 Pour some sprinkles onto a plate. Spread a very thin layer of cream around the sides of a cake. Roll the sides in the sprinkles. Put the cake on a plate. Do the same with the other cakes.

10 Spoon the remaining cream into your piping bag or gun. Pipe a flat spiral onto each cake – see page 53 for tips. Or, just spread on the cream.

Other ideas

Instead of making little cakes, you could bake the mixture in a 27 x 18cm (11 x 7in) rectangular tin for 30-35 minutes. Cool on a wire rack. Spread the apricot cream on top, scatter on some sprinkles and cut into 12-15 squares.

You could decorate your cakes with paper cake toppers. Find out how to make them on page 21.

Paper decorations

Here you'll find instructions for making different types of paper flags, cake toppers and other paper decorations. They look great on birthday cakes, but you could adapt them for other types of party cakes, too.

Flags on a string

You will need a strip of patterned paper around 6cm (2½in) wide and 24cm (9in) long, a ruler, pencil, scissors, glue, a long piece of string and two wooden skewers or lollipop sticks.

1 Fold the strip of paper in half lengthwise, with the pattern on the inside. Use the ruler and pencil to mark it into 12 strips, each 2cm (¾in) wide.

2 Cut out the strips and unfold them. Lay them out patterned side down in a straight line, spaced a little way apart. Spread some glue on each one.

3 Lay the string across the middle of the strips, with a long end at each side. Fold the top halves of the strips down onto the bottom halves. Leave to dry.

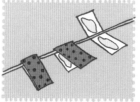

You could tie *ribbon bows* to the tops of the sticks.

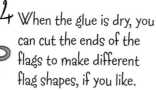

4 When the glue is dry, you can cut the ends of the flags to make different flag shapes, if you like.

5 Tie the ends of the string to the tops of the skewers or lollipop sticks. Push the bottom ends into a cake.

For shaped flags like these, follow steps 1-2 of the instructions below, but lay a long ribbon over the backs of all the shapes.

Stick the ribbon to the back of each shape with sticky tape.

Cake toppers

You will need some patterned paper, shapes to draw around such as little cookie cutters or coins, a pencil, scissors, 12 cocktail sticks and some sticky tape.

1 Put the paper on a surface, patterned side down. Put on the cookie cutters or coins and draw around them so you have 12 shapes.

2 Cut out the shapes. Lay them patterned side down. Put a cocktail stick over each one, so the point of the stick is in the middle of the shape.

3 Stick sticky tape over each cocktail stick, to stick it to the paper shape. Then, push the toppers into your cakes.

To make mini cake flags like these, follow the steps for making flags on the opposite page, but instead of string, lay a cocktail stick across each strip.

Confetti

Decorate your table with confetti made by punching through coloured paper with an ordinary hole punch – or a shaped hole punch, if you have one.

A heart-shaped hole punch

White chocolate strawberry cake

Ingredients:

125g (4½oz) caster sugar

125g (4½oz) softened butter or margarine

3 medium eggs

2 teaspoons milk

125g (4½oz) self-raising flour

1 teaspoon baking powder

For the chocolate-drizzled strawberries (optional):

150g (5oz) fresh strawberries

50g (2oz) white chocolate

For the white chocolate mousse:

150g (5oz) white chocolate

300ml (½ pint) whipping cream

For the filling:

4 tablespoons strawberry jam

1 tablespoon lemon juice

You will also need two 20cm (8in) round, shallow cake tins and a piping gun or bag fitted with a tiny, round nozzle.

Makes 12 slices

This soft sponge cake is topped and filled with white chocolate and strawberry mousse. You can decorate the cake with strawberries drizzled in white chocolate, too.

1 Heat the oven to 180°C, 350°F or gas mark 4. Grease and line the tins – see page 6.

2 Put the sugar and butter or margarine in a big bowl. Crack an egg into a cup. Tip it into the bowl. Do the same with the other eggs.

3 Add the milk and mix well. Sift on the flour and baking powder and mix them in gently.

When the cakes are cool, peel off the parchment.

4 Divide the mixture between the tins. Level the tops with the back of a spoon. Bake for 20-25 minutes or until risen and firm.

5 Leave the cakes for a few minutes, then turn them onto a wire rack to cool.

6 To make the chocolate-drizzled strawberries, cover a plate with baking parchment. Arrange the strawberries on it, lying on their sides, so they aren't touching.

7 Melt the chocolate (see page 27). Spoon it into the piping gun or bag.

8 Pipe a zigzag line over each strawberry, following the instructions on page 13. Then, put the plate in the fridge.

Instead of using fresh strawberries, you could double the amount of jam and marble it through the topping as well as the filling.

9 To make the mousse, melt the chocolate (see page 27). Wearing oven gloves, lift the bowl out of the pan. Leave to cool.

Don't beat too much, or the cream will go hard.

10 Pour the cream into a bowl. Whisk it very quickly, until it stays in a floppy point when you lift up the whisk.

Move the spoon in the...

...shape of a number 8.

11 Put a large spoonful of the cream onto the melted chocolate. Fold it in gently, using a big metal spoon. Add the rest of the cream. Fold in gently.

12 To make the filling, mix the jam and lemon juice in a bowl. Spoon in half the mousse. Mix gently. Stop when it looks marbled.

13 Put one cake on a serving plate. Spoon on the filling. Put the other cake on top. Spoon on the remaining mousse. Top with the berries. Refrigerate for 1 hour.

Other flavours

You could make a white chocolate cherry or raspberry cake instead. Just swap the fruit and the jam.

Party cupcakes

Ingredients:

125g (4½oz) butter or margarine

2 medium eggs

150g (5oz) caster sugar

200g (7oz) self-raising flour

100g (4oz) chocolate chips (optional)

75ml (3floz) milk

For the buttercream:

100g (4oz) softened butter or margarine

225g (8oz) icing sugar

1 tablespoon milk or water

1 teaspoon vanilla essence

different shades of food dye

For the chocolate sauce:

40g (1½oz) plain or milk chocolate

75ml (3floz) double cream

You will also need a 12-hole deep muffin tin, 12 paper muffin cases, some sugar sprinkles and some cake toppers (see page 21).

Makes 12

These simple cupcakes make a great party activity. Bake them in advance, then let your party guests add buttercream, sauce, sprinkles and cake toppers.

1 Heat the oven to 180°C, 350°F or gas mark 4. Put a paper case in each hole of the muffin tray.

2 Put the butter or margarine in a small pan. Heat gently until it melts. Leave it to cool.

3 Break an egg into a cup, then tip it into a bowl. Break the other egg into the cup. Tip it into the bowl. Beat with a fork.

4 Put the sugar in a big bowl. Sift on the flour. Add the chocolate chips. Mix. Add the milk, eggs and butter or margarine. Mix well.

5 Divide the mixture between the paper cases. Bake for 12-15 minutes, until risen and firm. Leave for 10 minutes, then put them on a wire rack to cool completely.

6 For the buttercream, put the butter or margarine in a bowl. Sift on one third of the icing sugar. Beat until soft. Sift on the rest of the icing sugar.

7 Add the milk or water and the vanilla. Beat until fluffy. Divide the buttercream between several bowls. Mix some food dye into each portion.

8 For the sauce, break up the chocolate. Put the cream in a small pan. Heat gently until it starts to steam. Take it off the heat. Add the chocolate, and stir until it melts.

9 Put out the cakes, bowls of buttercream, sauce, sprinkles and cake toppers. Your guests can spoon some buttercream onto a cupcake, pour on some sauce and then add sprinkles and toppers.

Other ideas

You could buy chocolate sauce – or other sauces such as toffee or strawberry.

For chocolate cupcakes, follow the cake recipe on pages 14-15, but spoon it into 15 muffin cases in two 12-hole deep muffin tins. Bake for 12-15 minutes.

Decorating basics

All through this book, you'll find instructions for creating different types of cake decorations. The tips here will help you with some basic techniques you'll need before you start making them.

 Marzipan contains nuts

Dyeing marzipan or icing

You will need some bought 'white' marzipan or white ready-to-roll icing and some food dye (for strong shades, use gel food dye).

1 Take a golf-ball sized blob of marzipan or icing. Make a hollow in the middle. Drop in 3 or 4 drops of food dye.

2 Fold the marzipan or icing over the dye. Keep on folding and squashing until the dye is evenly mixed through.

Rolling out

1 To roll out marzipan or ready-to-roll icing, dust a surface and a rolling pin with a little icing sugar.

2 Use the rolling pin to roll out the marzipan or icing until it's around 2mm ($\frac{1}{8}$in) thick. Then, cut it into shapes using a knife or tiny cookie cutters.

Melting chocolate

You will need a heatproof bowl that fits snugly in a saucepan. The bottom of the bowl shouldn't touch the bottom of the pan.

1 Fill the pan a quarter full of water. Put it over a medium heat. When the water bubbles, take the pan off the heat.

2 Break up the chocolate and put it in the bowl. Wearing oven gloves, carefully lower the bowl into the pan.

3 Leave for 5 minutes. Then, stir until the chocolate melts. Wearing oven gloves, remove the bowl from the pan.

Using sprinkles

Sugar sprinkles and strands will stick to your cakes better before the icing dries. So if you're using them, add them straight away.

Cake ribbons

If you'd like to decorate a cake with ribbon, it's best not to ice the sides of the cake, or the ribbon will get sticky. Put the ribbon around the cake, with the ends at the back. Stick the top end over the bottom end, using sticky tape.

Chocolate curl cake

Ingredients:

300g (11oz) plain or milk chocolate

125g (4½oz) butter

1½ tablespoons golden syrup

150g (5oz) plain biscuits such as digestives

75g (3oz) ready-to-eat dried fruit such as raisins or apricots

75g (3oz) glacé cherries

75g (3oz) unsalted nuts such as hazelnuts or almonds (optional)

For the chocolate frosting:

50g (2oz) butter

100g (4oz) plain or milk chocolate

For decorating:

a block of plain or milk chocolate, at room temperature

lots of chocolate finger biscuits

You will also need an 18cm (7in) or 15cm (6in) round, deep cake tin, a heatproof bowl that fits snugly into a saucepan, and a y-shaped vegetable peeler.

Makes 14-16 slices

This recipe doesn't involve any baking. You just make a chocolate biscuit cake that sets in the fridge, and decorate it with finger biscuits and chocolate curls. For a nut-free version, just leave out the nuts.

1 For the cake, line the sides and base of the cake tin with plastic food wrap. Leave the edges of the wrap hanging over the sides of the tin.

2 Break the chocolate into squares and cut the butter into chunks. Put them in the heatproof bowl. Add the golden syrup, too.

3 Fill the saucepan a quarter full with water. Heat until the water bubbles. Take it off the heat. Wearing oven gloves, lower in the bowl. Leave for 2 minutes.

4 Stir until the chocolate and butter are melted and smooth. Wearing oven gloves, take the bowl out of the pan. Leave it to cool.

5 Break the biscuits into small pieces. Put them in the bowl. Cut up any large dried fruits. Add the fruit, cherries and nuts. Stir well.

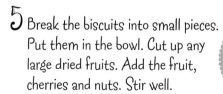

6 Scrape it into the cake tin. Level the top with the back of a spoon. Put it in the fridge for at least 2 hours.

7 To make the frosting, melt the butter in a small pan. Take it off the heat. Stir in the chocolate. Put it in a bowl in the fridge for 30 minutes.

Peel off the food wrap before you frost the cake.

8 To make the chocolate curls, scrape the vegetable peeler along the side of the chocolate block. Let the curls fall into a bowl.

9 Take the cake out of the tin. Put it on a serving plate. Spread frosting over the sides of the cake. Spread a little on top, too.

10 Press finger biscuits around the sides of the cake. Scatter the curls into the middle, straight from the bowl.

You could replace the nuts or cherries, and the curls, with malted chocolate balls, marshmallows, or chopped soft fudge.

29

Pink layer cake

This spectacular layer cake in shades of pink is filled and topped with vanilla cream. Each of the layers is made separately, and baked one after the other.

Ingredients:

around 200g (7oz) plain flour

2¼ teaspoons baking powder

150g (5oz) caster sugar

6 tablespoons sunflower oil

6 teaspoons vanilla essence

a little milk

pink liquid food dye

6 medium eggs

a little cream of tartar

For the vanilla cream:

300ml (½ pint) double or whipping cream

2 tablespoons icing sugar

1 teaspoon vanilla essence

You will also need a 20cm (8in) round, shallow cake tin.

Makes 14-18 slices

1 Heat the oven to 170°C, 325°F, gas mark 3. Cut a circle of baking parchment to fit the bottom of the tin (see page 6), then cut two more the same. Grease and line the tin.

2 Sift 65g (2½oz) of flour and ¾ teaspoon of baking powder into a big bowl. Add 75g (3oz) of sugar and stir it in.

3 Put 2 tablespoons of sunflower oil, 2 teaspoons of vanilla, 5½ teaspoons of milk and ½ teaspoon of food dye in a jug.

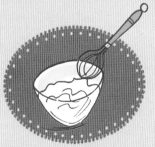

4 Separate 2 eggs. Put the whites in a large bowl. Put the yolks in the jug and beat with a fork.

5 Sprinkle a pinch of cream of tartar over the egg whites. Whisk until they become thick and foamy. The foam should stay in a point when you lift the whisk.

6 Pour the oil and milk mixture into the flour mixture. Mix well. Spoon in one third of the egg whites.

Move the spoon in the...

...shape of a number 8.

7 Use a spatula or metal spoon to fold them in gently. Add the rest of the egg whites. Fold until just mixed. Scrape into the tin.

8 Bake for 20 minutes. Test with a skewer (page 7) to make sure it's cooked. Leave for 5 minutes. Turn the cake onto a wire rack. Wash and dry the tin.

9 Grease and line the tin again. Follow step 2. Put 2 tablespoons of sunflower oil, 2 teaspoons of vanilla, 4 teaspoons of milk and 2 teaspoons of food dye in the jug. Follow steps 4-8.

Use the same bowls and jug — you don't need to wash them.

10 Grease and line the tin again. Follow step 2. Put 2 tablespoons of sunflower oil, 2 teaspoons of vanilla, 3 teaspoons of milk and 3 teaspoons of food dye in a jug. Follow steps 4-8.

Don't beat too much, or it will go hard.

Decorate the top with sugar sprinkles if you like.

11 For the vanilla cream, pour the cream into a bowl. Sift on the icing sugar and add the vanilla. Whisk until the cream stands in a floppy point when you lift the whisk.

12 When the cakes are cold, put one on a board. Use a sharp knife to trim off the browned edges all the way around. Do the same with the other cakes.

13 Put the first cake on a serving plate. Spread on one third of the cream. Put the second cake on top. Spread on half the remaining cream. Put the third cake on top and spread on the rest of the cream.

Butterfly cake

Ingredients:

300g (11oz) plain flour

2½ teaspoons baking powder

2½ teaspoons ground cinnamon

½ teaspoon ground mace (optional)

a pinch ground allspice (optional)

150g (5oz) soft dark brown sugar

175ml (6floz) sunflower
  or vegetable oil

5 medium eggs

2 ripe, medium-sized bananas

1 tablespoon lemon juice

a 400g (14oz) can of crushed
  pineapple

For the frosting:

300g (11oz) full-fat cream
  cheese

125g (4½oz) icing sugar

For decorating:

coloured butterflies (see page 35)

You will also need a 20cm (8in)
round, deep cake tin.

Makes 12-14 slices

This cake is packed with pineapple and banana, making it really moist and juicy. It's topped with coloured butterflies. Find out how to make them on page 35.

1 Heat the oven to 180°C, 350°F or gas mark 4. Grease and line the tin (see page 6). Take the cream cheese out of the fridge.

2 Sift the flour, baking powder, cinnamon, mace and allspice into a big bowl. Add the sugar and stir it in.

3 Put the oil in a bowl. Break an egg into a cup, then tip it into the oil. Do the same with each of the other eggs. Beat with a fork.

4 Peel the bananas and put them on a plate. Mash them with a fork or potato masher. Stir in the lemon juice. Then add the banana mixture to the oil mixture.

5 Set aside 1½ tablespoons of pineapple from the can. Tip the rest of the contents of the can into the oil mixture. Mix, then pour this into the flour mixture. Mix well. Scrape it into the tin.

When the cake is cool, peel off the parchment.

6 Bake for 55-60 minutes, until risen and springy. Test with a skewer. Leave in the tin for 10 minutes. Turn it onto a wire rack. Leave until completely cold.

Don't beat too hard, or it will go watery.

7 For the frosting, put the cream cheese in a big bowl. Beat until smooth. Sift on the icing sugar. Add the pineapple you set aside. Mix gently.

8 Put the cake on a serving plate. Spread the frosting over the top and sides, making peaks and swirls as you spread it on.

9 Push half a butterfly a little way into the frosting, at an angle. Push the other half in next to it, so it looks as if the butterfly is opening its wings.

Butterfly & nest decorations

Here you'll find out how to pipe summery coloured butterflies to decorate the butterfly cake on pages 32-33. There are also instructions for making chocolate nests, which would suit spring party cakes.

Chocolate nests

You will need 12 eggs in eggboxes, some plastic food wrap, 75g (3oz) plain chocolate, a heatproof bowl that fits snugly into a pan, a piping gun or bag fitted with a tiny, round nozzle, and some mini chocolate eggs.

1 Cut a square of food wrap. Drape the middle over one end of an egg. Smooth the wrap down the egg, bunching it up at the other end of the egg, to secure it.

2 Put the egg back in the box with the smooth end up. Wrap the other eggs in the same way.

3 Melt the chocolate (see page 27). Spoon it into the piping gun or bag. Pipe scribbly lines over and around the top of each egg – see page 13 for tips on piping lines.

4 Refrigerate for 30 minutes. Very carefully unwrap the food wrap from each egg and peel off the nests. Put them on cakes. Fill with mini chocolate eggs.

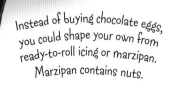

Instead of buying chocolate eggs, you could shape your own from ready-to-roll icing or marzipan. Marzipan contains nuts.

These bright butterflies were made using gel food dye. Liquid food dye will give you paler butterflies.

This is the chocolate cake from page 14, topped and filled with vanilla buttercream (page 24).

Butterfly decorations

You will need a chopping board, some baking parchment, 75g (3oz) white chocolate, a heatproof bowl that fits snugly into a pan, some food dye and a piping gun or bag fitted with a tiny, round nozzle.

1 Cut some parchment to fit your board. Place the parchment over the butterfly templates on pages 60-61. Trace over them with a pencil.

2 Move the parchment along and trace over them again, until you have around 20 butterflies. Turn over the parchment. Stick it to the board with sticky tape.

3 Melt the chocolate (see page 27). Take the bowl out of the pan. Stir in a few drops of food dye. Don't add too much dye, or it might make the chocolate harden.

If they soften, put them back in the fridge.

4 Spoon the chocolate into the gun or bag. Pipe over the pencil butterflies – see page 13 for tips. Refrigerate them for 15 minutes. Unstick the parchment. Peel off the butterflies.

5 Take half a butterfly. Push the body part into some frosting, with the wing tips sticking up. Add the other half, so it looks as if the butterfly is opening its wings.

Stripey cake

Ingredients:

15g (½oz) unsalted butter

4 tablespoons cocoa powder

1½ tablespoons soft light brown sugar

300ml (½ pint) plain natural yogurt

225g (8oz) softened butter or margarine

300g (11oz) caster sugar

6 medium eggs

350g (12oz) plain flour

1 teaspoon baking powder

½ teaspoon bicarbonate of soda

2 tablespoons vanilla essence

For the decorating:

25g (1oz) white chocolate

25g (1oz) plain chocolate

You will also need a fluted ring tin with a capacity of at least 2.5 litres (5 pints), a pastry brush and a piping gun or bag fitted with a tiny, round nozzle, plus a spare bag. To measure capacity, fill the tin with water, then measure it into a jug.

Makes around 20 slices

This recipe is for a moist, ring-shaped cake with wavy chocolate and vanilla stripes. The stripes are made by putting the cake mix into the tin in an unusual way.

1 Melt the unsalted butter in a small pan over a gentle heat. Brush it all over the inside of the tin. Measure out all the ingredients. Heat the oven to 180°C, 350°F or gas mark 4.

2 Sift the cocoa powder and soft light brown sugar into a bowl. Add 5 tablespoons of the yogurt and mix well.

3 Put the butter or margarine and caster sugar in a big bowl. Beat until fluffy. Break an egg into a cup. Tip it into the bowl. Add 1 teaspoon of the flour. Mix well.

4 Add the other eggs one at a time, in the same way. Then, sift in the rest of the flour with the baking powder and bicarbonate of soda.

5 Fold in gently. When the flour is half mixed in, add the rest of the yogurt and the vanilla. Fold again until mixed. Mix one third of the vanilla mixture into the cocoa mixture.

6 Drop 5 heaped teaspoons of the vanilla mixture into the tin, spaced evenly around the central post. Use the back of the spoon to spread them out, so they join up in a rough ring shape.

The rings won't reach to the edge of the tin, but this is fine.

7 Drop 4 teaspoons of chocolate mixture on top, and spread them into a ring too. Try not to mix the chocolate into the vanilla.

Don't worry if the layers look messy or uneven.

8 Keep on adding alternate layers of vanilla and chocolate mixture in the same way, until they are both used up.

9 Bake for 55-60 minutes, or until risen and firm. Test with a skewer to see if it's cooked (see page 7).

10 Put the tin on a wire rack for 15 minutes, then turn the cake out of the tin onto the wire rack. Leave to cool completely.

11 Melt the white chocolate (page 27). Spoon it into the piping gun or bag. Pipe a zigzag over the cake. Wash the gun or change the bag. Repeat with the plain chocolate.

Other shapes

You can make this recipe in a 20cm (8in) round, deep tin with a loose base. Grease and line the tin. Halve the quantities. At step 7, drop alternate tablespoonfuls of the mixtures into the middle of the tin, one on top of the other. Don't spread them out. Bake for 30-40 minutes.

Ice cream cake

Ingredients:

50g (2oz) plain chocolate

1 medium egg

65g (2½oz) softened butter or margarine

125g (4½oz) soft brown sugar

25g (1oz) self-raising flour

15g (½oz) plain flour

1 tablespoon cocoa powder

1½ litres (2½ pints) ice cream, or 2 litres (4 pints) soft-scoop ice cream

You will also need a 20cm (8in) square cake tin, a heatproof bowl that fits snugly into a saucepan and a 900g (2lb) loaf tin, measuring around 20½ x 12½ x 8cm (8 x 5 x 3½in).

Makes 10 slices

To make this cake, you bake a chocolate brownie and then sandwich it between layers of ice cream. You can use whatever flavour (or flavours) of ice cream you like.

1 Heat the oven to 180°C, 350°F or gas mark 4. Grease and line the square cake tin. Melt the chocolate, following the instructions on page 27.

2 Break the egg into a cup. Beat it with a fork. Put the butter and sugar into a big bowl. Beat until fluffy.

3 Add a spoonful of egg and beat it in. Add the rest of the egg a spoonful at a time, beating well each time.

4 Sift both types of flour and the cocoa into the bowl. Add the melted chocolate. Mix well. Spoon into the tin. Spread it out with the back of a spoon.

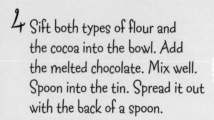

5 Bake for 20 minutes, until slightly risen with a crust on top. Leave in the tin to cool. When it is cold, take the ice cream out of the freezer and leave it for 10 minutes.

6 Run a knife around the brownie and shake it onto a board. Turn it the right way up. Use a sharp knife to cut off the raised edges. Then, cut the brownie in half.

You can eat the edges later – they're delicious!

Chocolate sauce

You will need 40g (1½oz) plain or milk chocolate and 75ml (3floz) double or whipping cream. To make the sauce, follow step 8 on page 25.

7 Line the loaf tin with a big piece of plastic food wrap. Leave the ends of the wrap hanging over the sides of the tin.

8 Fill the tin one third full of ice cream. Push it into the corners and pack it down well. Then, smooth the top with the back of a spoon.

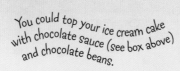

You could top your ice cream cake with chocolate sauce (see box above) and chocolate beans.

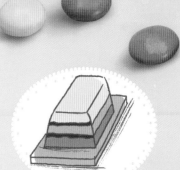

Don't worry if the brownie breaks – piece it back together in the tin.

9 Put one half of the brownie on top. You may need to trim the end off to make it fit. Spoon in more ice cream so the tin is two-thirds full. Smooth the top.

10 Put the other piece of brownie on top. Trim it if you need to. Add more ice cream to fill the tin. Smooth the top. Fold the ends of food wrap over the top. Freeze for at least 4 hours.

11 Peel the food wrap off the top. Put the tin upside down on a board. Rub a hot, damp cloth over the outside of the tin. The cake will pop out. Remove the tin and the food wrap.

Coconut cake

Ingredients:

200g (7oz) butter or margarine

3 medium eggs

6 tablespoons desiccated coconut

225g (8oz) caster sugar

300g (11oz) self-raising flour

120ml (4floz) milk

For the frosting:

300g (11oz) full-fat cream cheese

100g (4oz) icing sugar

½ teaspoon coconut essence (optional)

For decorating:

2 tablespoons desiccated coconut

pink food dye

3 tablespoons seedless raspberry jam

1 teaspoon lemon juice

You will also need a 27 x 18cm (11 x 7in) rectangular cake tin.

Makes 12-15 squares

Other ideas

You could use other flavours of jam such as apricot or blueberry. Dye the coconut to match the jam.

This soft coconut traybake is spread with cream cheese frosting and then topped with raspberry sauce and pink desiccated coconut.

1 Take the cream cheese out of the fridge. Heat the oven to 180°C, 350°F or gas mark 4. Grease and line the tin (see page 6).

2 Heat the butter or margarine gently in a small pan until it melts. Leave to cool.

3 Break an egg into a cup, then tip it into a small bowl. Do the same with the other eggs. Beat them with a fork.

4 Put the coconut and sugar in a big bowl. Sift in the flour. Mix. Add the milk, eggs and butter. Mix well.

5 Pour and scrape the mixture into the tin. Bake for 20-30 minutes, or until risen and firm. Test it with your finger (see page 7).

6 Leave the cake for 10 minutes. Then, run a knife around the edge of the tin and turn the cake onto a wire rack. Leave it to cool completely.

When the cake is cool, peel off the parchment.

Don't beat too much, or it will go watery.

7 To make the frosting, put the cream cheese in a big bowl. Beat until smooth. Sift on the icing sugar. Add the coconut essence. Mix gently.

8 For the pink coconut, put the coconut in a small bowl. Add a few drops of food dye and mix it in really well with a teaspoon.

9 For the sauce, push the jam though a sieve into a bowl. Scrape the jam off the back of the sieve, too. Mix in the lemon juice. Add a few drops of pink food dye too, if you like.

10 Put the cake on a board. Spread the frosting over the top. Scoop up some sauce on a teaspoon. Drizzle it over the cake in a zigzag shape. Then, scatter over the coconut.

You could pipe on the sauce using a piping bag or gun fitted with a tiny round nozzle.

This cake was decorated with coconut and raspberry flavoured jelly beans.

Gingerbread cake

Ingredients:

275g (10oz) golden syrup

100g (4oz) dark muscovado sugar

100g (4oz) butter

225g (8oz) self-raising flour

1 tablespoon ground ginger

1 teaspoon ground cinnamon

2 medium eggs

2 tablespoons milk

For decorating:

100g (4oz) icing sugar

You will also need a 900g (2lb) loaf tin, measuring around 20 x 12 x 8cm (8 x 5 x 3½in).

Makes around 12 slices

This soft, loaf-shaped cake is flavoured with ginger, syrup, and brown sugar. If you keep it for a few days, it will become deliciously moist and sticky.

1 Heat the oven to 170°C, 325°F or gas mark 3. Grease and line the tin (see page 6).

2 Put the syrup, sugar and butter in a saucepan. Put it over a low heat. Stir now and then, until the butter melts. Take it off the heat.

3 Sift the flour, ginger and cinnamon into big bowl. Make a hollow in the middle.

4 Break an egg into a cup. Tip the egg into a jug. Do the same with the other egg. Add the milk and beat with a fork until mixed.

5 Pour the syrup mixture into the flour. Start mixing. When half the flour is mixed in, add the egg mixture. Keep stirring until everything is well mixed.

The top of the cake may crack but this doesn't matter.

6 Pour the mixture into the tin. Bake for 50 minutes. Test with a skewer to check it is cooked.

When the cake is cool, peel off the parchment.

7 Leave to cool for 15 minutes, then turn the cake out of the tin onto a wire rack. Leave it upside down to cool.

8 To make the icing, sift the icing sugar into a bowl. Add 1 tablespoon of cold water and mix to a smooth paste.

9 Spoon the icing over the cake, so it dribbles down the sides (see page 12). Wait until it dries before you add any decorations.

Other flavours

For a richer, darker flavour, use just 200g (7oz) golden syrup and add 75g (3oz) black treacle at the same time.

For a zesty icing, replace the water with lemon or lime juice.

You'll find instructions on page 44 for making houses like these, to decorate your cake.

This roof was decorated with patterns piped in glittery writing icing.

For a snowy roof, spread on white writing icing, then scatter on white sprinkles or sparkling sugar.

Add details like these using the side or end of a cocktail stick.

You could scatter sparkling sugar on top of your cake and serving plate.

House & star decorations

Here you will find out how to make little houses to decorate the gingerbread cake on pages 42-43. There are also icing candy canes and white chocolate snowflakes. They all make great decorations for winter party cakes.

Marzipan contains nuts

House decorations

You will need a rolling pin, icing sugar and red, blue, brown and white marzipan or ready-to-roll icing (see page 26 – for brown marzipan or icing, knead in 1 teaspoon of cocoa powder instead of food dye).

1 Take a golf-ball sized blob of icing or marzipan. Shape it into a rough cube. Pat it against a clean, flat surface to make the sides flat.

2 Put the cube down. Pinch and squash two of the sides together into a point to make a roof on top of the cube, like this.

3 Dust a clean surface and a rolling pin with a little icing sugar. Roll out some white marzipan or icing until it is half as thick as a pencil.

4 Cut 2 rectangles. Each one should fit over one side of the roof. They should meet at the middle. Put them on and pat gently into place.

5 Use small pieces of icing or marzipan to shape a chimney, a door, a door handle and a window. Pat them on.

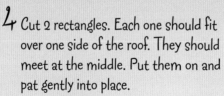

To edge a roof, cut 2 strips of white icing. Use a cutter with a wavy edge to shape one side of each strip.

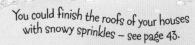

You could finish the roofs of your houses with snowy sprinkles – see page 43.

Chocolate stars

You will need 40g (1½oz) white chocolate and 40g (1½oz) plain or milk chocolate, a chopping board, some baking parchment, sticky tape and a piping gun or bag fitted with a tiny, round nozzle.

1 Follow steps 1-2 on page 35, but trace over the star templates (page 58-59) until you have around 20 shapes. Melt the white chocolate, following the steps on page 27.

2 Spoon the chocolate into the piping gun or bag. Pipe it over half the pencil stars (see page 13 for tips on piping lines). Wash and dry the nozzle. Attach it to a clean, dry gun or a fresh piping bag.

If they soften, put them back in the fridge.

3 Make the plain chocolate stars in the same way. Put the board in the fridge for 15 minutes. Then, unstick the parchment. Very carefully, peel off a star. Push it into the frosting on a cake.

For candy canes, roll two sticks of icing or marzipan, one red and one white. Twist them together, roll again, then bend one end over.

As well as templates for stars, you'll find other shapes, including snowflakes, on pages 58-59.

Strawberry jam cake

Ingredients:

1 lemon

175g (6oz) smooth strawberry jam

2 tablespoons red food dye

225g (8oz) softened butter or margarine

175g (6oz) caster sugar

275g (10oz) self-raising flour

4 medium eggs

1 teaspoon baking powder

For the buttercream:

150g (5oz) softened butter or margarine

75g (3oz) smooth strawberry jam

1 tablespoon lemon juice

250g (9oz) icing sugar

For decorating:

2 tablespoons smooth strawberry jam

a few drops of red food dye

You will also need a 20cm (8in) round, deep cake tin, a skewer and a cocktail stick.

Makes 14-16 slices

This moist cake has strawberry jam in every bit of it. The cake has jam baked into it. The icing is strawberry jam buttercream and the decorations are shiny jam hearts.

1 Heat the oven to 180°C, 350°F or gas mark 4. Grease and line the tin (see page 6).

2 Grate the zest from the lemon on the fine holes of a grater. Mix the zest, jam and food dye in a small bowl. Squeeze the juice from the lemon and set it aside.

3 Put the butter or margarine and sugar in a big bowl. Beat until fluffy. Add the jam mixture and 1 tablespoon of the flour. Beat well.

4 Break the eggs into a cup. Beat with a fork. Tip into the big bowl. Sift in the rest of the flour and the baking powder. Stir until smooth. Spoon into the tin.

5 Bake for 45 minutes, then cover with kitchen foil. Bake for 10-15 minutes more. Push a skewer into the middle. If it comes out clean, the cake is cooked. If not, cook for 10 more minutes, then test again.

6 Leave the cake for 15 minutes. Remove it from the tin (see page 7). Put it on a wire rack to cool.

When the cake is cool, peel off the parchment.

7 For the buttercream, put the butter or margarine in a big bowl. Add the jam and lemon juice and beat until fluffy. Sift in the icing sugar. Mix well.

8 When the cake is cool, put it on a serving plate. Spread the buttercream over the sides and top of the cake. Smooth the surface with a blunt knife.

9 To decorate the cake, push the jam though a sieve into a bowl. Scrape the jam off the back of the sieve, too. Mix in the food dye and 1 teaspoon of lemon juice.

10 Use a cocktail stick to mark three circles, one inside the other, on the cake. Drop ¼ teaspoon of the jam mixture onto one of the circles.

11 Drop more blobs all along the circles, 2½cm (1in) apart. Drag the point of the cocktail stick along each circle, through the blobs of jam. They will become hearts.

You could use other jam flavours, such as apricot or cherry. Choose a food dye to match.

Lemon cake

Ingredients:

2 lemons

3 medium eggs

50g (2oz) softened butter or margarine

300g (11oz) caster sugar

250g (9oz) ricotta cheese

175g (6oz) self-raising flour

For the lemon buttercream:

1 lemon

200g (7oz) softened butter or margarine

350g (12oz) icing sugar

You will also need two 15cm (6in) round cake tins and a skewer.

Makes 12 slices

This tangy cake has a moist texture and is covered with luscious lemon buttercream. You could decorate it with cake flags – find out how to make them on page 20.

1 Heat the oven to 180°C, 350°F or gas mark 4. Grease and line the cake tins. Grate the zest from the lemons on the small holes of a grater. Cut one lemon in half and squeeze out the juice.

2 Separate the eggs (see page 8). Put the whites in a big, very clean bowl. Put the yolks in another big bowl.

3 Add the lemon zest, butter or margarine and sugar to the yolks. Mix well. Add a spoonful of ricotta. Mix it in with a fork. Add the rest of the ricotta a spoonful at a time, mixing each time.

Move the spoon in the...

...shape of a number 8.

4 Sift the flour over the ricotta mixture. Use a spatula or a big metal spoon to fold it in gently.

5 Whisk the egg whites until they are thick and foamy. The foam should stay in a point when you lift the whisk. Add the whites to the ricotta mixture. Fold them in gently.

6 Divide the mixture between the tins. Level the tops with the back of a spoon. Bake for 40-45 minutes until risen and firm. Test them with a finger (see page 7).

7 Put the tins on a wire rack. Poke holes all over the tops of the cakes with the skewer. Pour over the lemon juice. Leave them to cool.

Use the small holes on a grater.

8 For the buttercream, grate the zest from the lemon, then squeeze out the juice. Put the zest in a big bowl. Add the butter or margarine.

9 Sift on half the icing sugar. Mix well. Sift on the rest of the icing sugar. Add 1½ tablespoons of lemon juice. Beat until fluffy.

If you don't have two 15cm (6in) cake tins, use one deep 20cm (8in) round tin instead. Bake for 45-55 minutes.

These curls of lemon zest were made using a tool known as a zester.

After this cake was iced, a blunt knife was used to make stripes in the buttercream.

10 Put one cake on a plate. Spread on a quarter of the buttercream. Put the other cake on top, upside down. Spread the rest of the buttercream over the top and sides of the cake.

Little rose cakes

Ingredients:

1 lemon

175g (6oz) caster sugar

175g (6oz) softened butter
  or margarine

175g (6oz) self-raising flour

3 medium eggs

For the rose syrup:

1 tablespoon caster sugar

1 teaspoon rose water

For the rose buttercream:

150g (5oz) softened butter
  or margarine

350g (12oz) icing sugar

1 tablespoon lemon juice

2½ teaspoons rose water

pink food dye

You will also need a 12-hole deep
muffin tin, 12 paper muffin cases
and a piping bag fitted with a big
snowflake-shaped nozzle.

Makes 12

Piped two-tone buttercream roses make a spectacular topping for these little rose-flavoured cakes. You can make other flavours if you like – see the box opposite.

1 Heat the oven to 180°C, 350°F or gas mark 4. Put a paper case in each hole of the muffin tray. Grate the zest from the lemon on the small holes of a grater. Cut the lemon in half, squeeze out the juice and put it in a jug.

2 Put the lemon zest, sugar and butter or margarine in a big bowl. Beat until fluffy. Sift on the flour.

3 Break one egg into a cup, then add it to the mixture. Do the same with each of the other eggs. Mix until smooth. Spoon into the paper cases.

4 Bake for 20-25 minutes. While the cakes are baking, make the syrup. Stir the sugar and rose water into the lemon juice in the jug.

5 When the cakes are risen and firm, spoon a little syrup onto each one. Put them on a wire rack to cool.

6 To make the buttercream, put the butter or margarine in a bowl. Beat with a wooden spoon until it's smooth. Sift on half the icing sugar. Mix it in.

7 Sift on the rest of the icing sugar. Add the lemon juice and rose water. Beat until fluffy.

Other flavours

If you leave out the rose water, your cakes will taste lemony.

These cakes were all iced with different shades of pink buttercream.

8 Mix a few drops of food dye into the buttercream to make a pale pink shade. Put 1 tablespoon of buttercream in a small bowl. Mix in more dye, to make a strong pink shade.

9 Spoon the strong pink buttercream into the piping bag. Put the bag on a flat surface and flatten it with your hand, like this. Pull the bag open again. Spoon in the pale pink buttercream.

10 Pipe a rose onto each cake, starting in the middle. For tips on piping roses, see page 53.

Piping swirls & rosettes

On page 13 you'll find help with piping basics, such as how to fill a piping bag and how to pipe a line or dot. These pages show you about other piping techniques such as making swirls, rosettes and roses.

Piping rosettes

You will need a filled piping gun or bag fitted with a star- or flower-shaped nozzle.

1 Hold your piping bag or gun so the nozzle is around ⅓cm (¼in) from surface of the cake.

2 Squeeze until some icing comes out and touches the cake. Keep the nozzle in the same place and keep squeezing until a small rosette forms.

3 To finish the rosette, stop squeezing and lift the nozzle up and away quickly.

All the cakes on these pages were topped with buttercream. See pages 24-25 for a recipe.

Piping swirls

This technique is used for the cupcakes on pages 10-11. You'll need a filled piping gun or bag fitted with a star- or flower-shaped nozzle.

1 First, pipe a medium-sized rosette in the middle of a cupcake, following the instructions above.

2 Then, pipe a spiral, starting at the edge of the cake and going in and up, over the rosette. Lift up and away quickly to finish.

A flat spiral

A swirl

This piped rose has a 2-tone effect. To find out how to do this, see page 51.

A rosette

Piping roses

Follow these tips to pipe roses (pages 50-51). You will need a filled piping gun or bag fitted with a snowflake-shaped nozzle.

1 Pipe a spiral, starting in the middle of the cake, and going outwards and around.

2 When you reach the edge of the cake, stop squeezing and move the nozzle away quickly, to finish.

3 Wet your finger. Use it to push the end in gently, so it clings to the rest of the spiral.

Flat spirals

To pipe the toppings for the little apricot cakes on pages 18-19, you'll need a filled piping gun or bag fitted with a medium-sized star-shaped nozzle.

Follow the instructions for piping roses, to the left. Because the nozzle shape is different, you will get a flat swirl instead of a rose.

Trying out techniques

If you're testing a new piping technique, try it out on a clean plate first. When you're happy with your piping, scrape the frosting off the plate and use it again.

Changing nozzles

Different sizes and shapes of nozzle can give very different effects. If you're using a piping gun, it's easy to change nozzles halfway through your piping by undoing the end. You can't do this if you're using a piping bag, unless you have a gadget called a coupler. This lets you change nozzles easily.

Pumpkin cake

Ingredients:

a piece of pumpkin or squash weighing around 350g (12oz)

1 orange

175ml (12 tablespoons) sunflower oil

200g (7oz) soft light brown sugar

4 medium eggs

225g (8oz) self-raising flour

1 teaspoon baking powder

1 teaspoon bicarbonate of soda

3 teaspoons ground cinnamon

2 teaspoons ground ginger

¼ teaspoon ground nutmeg or mace (optional)

a pinch of ground cloves (optional)

100g (4oz) plain or milk chocolate chips

For the topping:

1 orange

50g (2oz) softened butter or margarine

100g (4oz) icing sugar

red and yellow food dye

100g (4oz) plain or milk chocolate

¼ teaspoon ground cinnamon

¼ teaspoon ground ginger

You will also need a 20cm (8in) round, deep cake tin.

Makes 12-16 slices

This cake is made with spices, chocolate chips and grated pumpkin. You can't really taste the pumpkin but it makes the cake extra light and moist.

1 Heat the oven to 180°C, 350°F or gas mark 4. Grease and line the tin (see page 6).

2 Use a vegetable peeler to peel the rind from the pumpkin. Scoop out the seeds with a spoon. Grate the pumpkin on the big holes of a grater. Stop when you have 250g (9oz).

3 Grate the rind from the outside of the orange on the small holes of a grater. Put it in a big bowl.

4 Put the oil and sugar in the bowl with the zest. Beat for a minute with a wooden spoon.

5 Break an egg into a cup. Tip it into the oil and sugar mixture and mix well. Do the same with each of the other eggs.

Move the spoon in the...

...shape of a number 8.

6 Add the grated pumpkin and mix it in. Sift in the flour, baking powder, bicarbonate of soda and spices. Tip in the chocolate chips.

7 Fold everything together gently with a spatula or a big metal spoon. Scrape into the tin. Bake for 50 minutes, until risen and firm. Test with a skewer (page 7).

When the cake is cool, peel off the parchment.

8 Leave in the tin for 10 minutes, then turn the cake onto a wire rack. Leave it upside down to cool completely.

9 For the topping, grate the zest from the orange on the small holes of a grater. Squeeze the juice from half the orange. Put half the zest in a big bowl and add the butter or margarine.

10 Beat until smooth. Sift in the icing sugar. Add 1½ teaspoons of the orange juice and a few drops of red and yellow food dye. Mix until orange and fluffy.

To make decorations like these, follow the instructions on page 57.

Pumpkin can be hard to cut up. Get someone to help you, or use the same amount of grated carrot or sweet potato instead.

11 Put the cake on a serving plate with the flat side up. Spread the orange frosting around the sides. Put the cake in the fridge.

12 Melt the chocolate (see page 27). Stir in the cinnamon, ginger and the remaining orange zest. Pour it on top of the cake – see page 12 for tips on drippy toppings.

Ghost & pumpkin decorations

Here you will find out how to make pumpkins to decorate the pumpkin cake on pages 54-55. There are also meringue ghosts and chocolate cobwebs. All of them make great decorations for spooky party cakes.

Meringue ghosts

You will need 2 medium eggs, 1 pinch cream of tartar (optional), 100g (4oz) caster sugar, 2 baking trays, a piping bag fitted with a large round nozzle and some chocolate writing icing.

1 Follow steps 1-6 of the meringue recipe on pages 16-17. Spoon some of the mixture into the piping bag. Pipe it onto the trays following the tips for piping rosettes and swirls on page 52.

2 Follow step 9 on page 17. When they are cold, draw on faces with the chocolate writing icing.

This ghost was piped in a swirl shape.

You could eat your ghosts on their own, or put them on a cake.

This ghost was piped in a rosette shape.

For chocolate cobwebs, follow the instructions for chocolate stars on page 45. You'll find cobweb templates on pages 60-61.

This is the chocolate cake from pages 14-15, with the whipped cream spread around the sides. It was topped with 100g (4oz) melted chocolate.

Marzipan contains nuts

Pumpkin decorations

You will need some whole cloves, a cocktail stick and red, yellow, green and brown marzipan or ready-to-roll icing (see page 26 for tips on dyeing marzipan or icing).

1 Squash and knead some red and yellow marzipan or icing together, to make orange. Roll some into a ball the size of a golf ball.

2 Put the point of the cocktail stick against the bottom of the ball. Tilt the stick up and over, so it makes a groove up the side of the ball, ending in the middle.

3 Make more grooves all the way around. Push your thumb into the middle of the ball, to make a dent.

4 Take a little green marzipan or icing. Roll it into a thin string. Wrap it around the cocktail stick to make a tendril. Push it off the end of the stick.

5 Take a clove. Remove the round part. Put the end of the tendril in the dent of the pumpkin. Use the divided end of the clove to spear it gently in place.

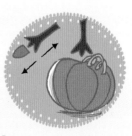

6 Use the brown marzipan or icing to shape eyes and a mouth. Push them on gently. They should stick.

For brown marzipan or icing, knead in a little cocoa powder instead of food dye.

These chocolate cupcakes were made using the recipe on pages 10-11.

Templates

These templates are for making piped chocolate decorations. For full instructions, see pages 35 and 45. When you pipe each shape, go along the lines shown in the lighter shade first, then fill in the darker lines.

A tiny star

Use the smaller shapes for decorating little cakes.

A medium snowflake

If you find these wavy lines hard to follow, just fill in the heart with squiggles.

These squiggles are just a guide – you could make up your own.

Small and medium hearts

Little butterflies

A cobweb

Pipe the two halves of each
butterfly separately.

Changing colours

The instructions on page 35 are for
colourful butterfly decorations, while
page 45 shows how to make plain and
white chocolate stars.

You could make coloured, plain or
white chocolate decorations in any of
the shapes. Follow the directions for
the shade of decorations you want to
make, using the shapes of templates
you prefer.

A tiny cobweb

A small butterfly

Medium cobwebs

A big butterfly

61

Index

Allergy advice

Some recipes in this book have ingredients marked as optional. Leave them out if you're cooking for someone who's allergic to them. There are suggestions in ingredients lists, boxes and captions for allergy-free ingredients you can use. The list below tells you about ingredients that might be a problem for those who can't eat wheat, gluten, dairy, egg or nuts. It also suggests ways of making recipes allergy-free.

If you're cooking for someone with food allergies, check any packaged ingredients, such as vanilla essence, jam, chocolate, baking powder, icing sugar, cocoa powder or sugar sprinkles, to make sure they don't contain anything unsuitable.

Sweetie cake
Contains wheat, gluten, dairy and egg.

Very chocolatey cupcakes
Contain dairy and egg.

Marshmallow & chocolate cake
Contains wheat, gluten, dairy and egg.

Multicoloured meringues
Contain egg.

Apricot sprinkle cakes
Contain wheat, gluten, dairy, egg and nuts. To make them wheat- and gluten-free, use cornmeal.

White chocolate strawberry cake
Contains wheat, gluten, dairy and egg.

Party cupcakes
Contain wheat, gluten, dairy and egg.

Chocolate curl cake
Contains wheat, gluten, dairy, egg and optional nuts.

Pink layer cake
Contains wheat, gluten, dairy and egg. To make it dairy-free, replace the whipped cream with vanilla buttercream (pages 24-25) made using dairy-free margarine and water instead of milk.

Butterfly cake
Contains wheat, gluten, dairy and egg. To make it dairy-free, replace the frosting with vanilla buttercream (pages 24-25) made using dairy-free margarine and water instead of milk.

Stripey cake
Contains wheat, gluten, dairy and egg.

Ice cream cake
Contains wheat, gluten, dairy and egg.

Coconut cake
Contains wheat, gluten, dairy, egg and coconut (coconut may not be suitable for nut allergy sufferers).

Gingerbread cake
Contains wheat, gluten, dairy and egg.

Strawberry jam cake
Contains wheat, gluten, dairy and egg. To make it dairy-free, use dairy-free margarine.

Lemon cake
Contains wheat, gluten, dairy and egg.

Little rose cakes
Contain wheat, gluten, dairy and egg. To make them dairy-free, use dairy-free margarine.

Pumpkin cake
Contains wheat, gluten, dairy and egg. To make it dairy-free, use dairy-free chocolate and margarine.

Art Director: Mary Cartwright   Senior designer: Helen Lee

Additional design by Alice Reese   Cover illustration by Antonia Miller   Digital imaging by Nick Wakeford & John Russell